The Kid Who Sold Money

The Kid Who Sold Money

DAN J. MARLOWE

GLOBE FEARON

Pearson Learning Group

FASTBACK® CRIME AND DETECTION BOOKS

Beginner's Luck

The Blind Alley

Fun World

The Kid Who Sold Money

The Lottery Winner

No Loose Ends

Return Payment

The Setup

Small-Town Beat

Snowbound

ISBN 0-13-024493-7

Printed in the United States of America

2 3 4 5 6 7 8 9 10   07 06 05

Globe
Fearon

Pearson Learning Group

1-800-321-3106
www.pearsonlearning.com

Joey Monohan parked his used car in the visitors' lot at the federal prison. He was dressed casually in a tank top and walking shorts. He had curly dark red hair and a batch of freckles sprinkled across his nose.

"Afternoon, Joey," the guard at the main desk said. He went through his file and pulled out the card on Joey's father, Charley Monohan.

Joey signed in. Then he joined the line of visitors waiting for the electric gate to open. It led to the metal detection unit that everyone had to pass through.

When Joey reached the visiting area, his father had not yet arrived. Joey found a chair off to one side. Charley always wanted to talk without being overheard. He said it was to keep the prison guards from learning about his escape plots. The plots were hatched with fellow inmates. But Charley and his friends would have had a hard time escaping from a church basement.

"Hi ya, kid," Charley said cheerfully as he walked into the room.

"Hi, Charley," Joey said, rising to his feet. He had always called his father Charley. The man was so seldom around that Dad or Pop never seemed to sound right.

Charley gave his son a quick handshake. He was not a man who showed his feelings very much. Like Joey, he had a slight frame—both were about five and a half feet and 140 pounds. Charley was, as always, red faced. Small patches of white hair stood out on both sides of his otherwise bald head.

"How's it going with you?" Charley asked after seating himself.

"Fine," Joey said, just the way he always did.

"Still working at the same place?"

Joey tried to remember what he had told his father about the last job he was supposed to have had. Was it the box boy at the supermarket? Or the manager for a string of newspaper carriers?

"The shipping room of the plastics factory?" Charley prompted him.

"No, I changed jobs." Joey spent five minutes making up a new job for himself as a drugstore clerk. "How's it going with you?" he asked finally.

"Three of us are going over the wall next month, kid," Charley told him. Joey nodded. Three, four, or five of them were always going over the wall next month. They never went. They never would. They were doing their time in a maximum security federal prison. And Charley Monohan wasn't there because of his track record of escapes. He was there because the U.S. Treasury Department liked to know where he was.

Joey smiled fondly at his father. Joey's mother had eased herself away from the Monohan home when Joey was six. She had left him only the soulful brown eyes which didn't seem to fit with the rest of his features. His father had raised the boy—if *raised* was the proper word.

During his regular stays in prison, Charley boarded Joey with friends or relatives. But from the age of 14, Joey spent long periods of time keeping house for himself. Some of

Charley's friends would knock on the apartment door monthly and silently hand him money for rent and food.

Joey had lived for the times when Charley was home. Their small, old kitchen was always filled with Charley's cigar-smoking pals. And Joey had listened to dozens of their plans for adding Charley's manufactured money to the government's regular supply.

Joey had known even during his teen years that none of the plans would work. It was exciting, though, to pretend they would. And sometimes they did, if only for a little while. Then life was *really* exciting.

"What's going on outside?" Charley asked him.

Joey knew his father was asking particularly about the outside world of counterfeiting. Through the years, Charley had made himself an expert at that "trade." That was why the Treasury Department insisted on making Charley's living arrangements.

"Not much of anything," Joey replied.

"Bunch of lazy bums out there!" Charley snorted. "I'll show them the next time I get the press running."

Joey nodded patiently. In one way, Charley's bragging wasn't an empty boast. His father's counterfeit money would pass anywhere, even at banks. The reason Charley's grand plans always broke down was his kitchen-table pals. They were the ones that passed the counterfeit bills Charley printed. And the first friend caught always led the Treasury agents right to Charley's front door.

After the second time that happened,

Joey had advised his father to slow down. He had urged Charley to run off no more than five or ten thousand at a time. Then the two of them could pass the bills themselves in small amounts. But Charley would have none of it. Nothing could stop him from filling boxes, cartons, and sometimes trunks with beautifully crisp twenties, fifties, and hundreds. He felt powerful when his press was running. He seemed to grow two inches taller when he was printing.

"I'll bust this darn government!" he would vow, his face turning even redder than usual. Charley was no voice of reason at those moments. Not that he was at other times, either.

"I'll show them . . . ," Charley said again to Joey. All this talk about his work reminded Charley of something. "What did you do with the stuff you had me run off last time?" he asked. "I still don't know how you talked me into it."

"A lot of it is still at the apartment," Joey said truthfully.

"Waste of good paper and ink," his father said.

Joey didn't reply. Instead, he asked if there was anything Charley needed. He shook his head. There never was. Charley had stopped smoking when he discovered that cigarette ash was damaging his plates.

Joey caught his father sneaking a look at the wall clock. Charley was getting restless. A 30-minute visit once a month was all that his active nature could stand. He liked to spend his prison time on other things. Like thinking up new counterfeiting and escape plans.

"Take care, Charley," Joey said, getting to his feet.

"You, too, kid," Charley answered, rising for another quick handshake. "Oh, yeah, how do I stand with the parole board?" Charley never bothered to keep track of it himself.

"You'll be up before them again in seven months," Joey told him. "I think you might make it then."

"That's if *I* don't give myself an earlier release time," Charley told him. He winked and said, "See ya next month, kid."

J oey drove the 40 miles back to their apartment in about an hour. He checked his watch as he opened the door. There was still time to get in a couple of hours' work. He removed one of Charley's loose-fitting business suits from the closet. He put it on right over his tank top and shorts. It was hot, but it was his working uniform.

He went into the bathroom and rubbed a powdery blond dye into his red hair. It lightened the color quite a bit. Makeup base applied to his nose covered his freckles. A pair of black-frame eyeglasses completed his new look.

He drove into town and parked in front of a bar. It was one he had scouted the night before. He always tried to choose places that did good business in the evenings. He wanted to talk with bartenders who had made good money the day before —and knew they would again.

Inside it was dimly lit. He waited until

his eyes adjusted to the darkness. The room was decorated with gold-framed mirrors, red carpeting, and black leather booths. Joey moved toward the long bar and sat down on a stool in front of the cash register.

At this hour, the place was nearly empty. There were no customers at the tables. And only two other drinkers were at the bar. One was a middle-aged woman three stools away who sat staring down into her drink. And at the far end, there was a man in a sharp-looking, light-colored suit. The man's face showed a look of total self-satisfaction.

The bartender came over and stopped in front of Joey. She looked at him, then looked again. "Maybe we can save each other's time if you show me your driver's license," she suggested. She was a tall woman with a deep voice.

"Sure," Joey said. "It happens everywhere I go." The license he removed from his wallet and handed over said he was Joseph Quisenbury, age 22. Joey had had a friend get him a fake license. It showed a picture of him the way he looked now—blondish hair, no freckles, glasses. And he had reasons for using a different last name. But the only item the woman was interested in was the one he didn't have to fake. He really was 22. The woman studied the license carefully, then examined Joey again. Finally she shrugged. "I still think you look too young, but you've got the paper. So . . . ? "

"So, I'm Joey," he said cheerfully with his best smile.

"Vicky," she returned.

"Hi, Vicky. I'd like the coldest beer you have in the bar. It's really hot outside when you've been pounding the pavement."

Vicky placed a bottle and a frosted glass in front of him. "Looking for a job—or out selling something?"

"I'm not looking for a job. I have one. I sell costume jewelry door-to-door."

Her world-weary eyes examined him again. "You don't really look like the type to be in something as foolish as door-to-door selling. I think beneath those glasses and that suit, there's a street-smart guy."

Joey almost choked on his first sip of beer. Was this woman too sharp to fall for his story? "You're not making me feel any better," he said.

"You're really trying to peddle stuff *downtown?*"

"They're breaking me in," Joey explained. "If I show good results here, I'll get one of the better routes in the suburbs." He raised his glass to her. "After the day I just had, this hits the spot."

"No sales?" she asked.

"Worse than that." Joey picked up his wallet from where it still rested on the bar. He took out a crisp new bill. "I learned something today. What was it someone once said? 'Education is what you get when you read the fine print, and experience is what you get when you don't.'

"Anyway, this customer made her choice

and stood there with money in her hand. She had a twenty on top. So, I made change for it. But when I got outside, I found she'd pulled back the twenty and given me this." He handed Vicky the bill.

"What is it?" she asked after checking her apron pocket for the glasses that weren't there. "A five? A one?"

"Take a look," Joey said.

Vicky found her glasses on the back bar and put them on. She held the bill under the light that hung above the register. "Say, now!" she exclaimed. "And here I thought I'd seen everything in the world twice!" She snapped the bill between her hands. It crackled loudly. "Sure sounds like the real thing." She was shaking her head when she turned back to Joey. "Tough luck, kid," she said. "You got taken by a pro."

Vicky placed the bill on the bar top. Their heads came together above it as though drawn by magnets. The bill looked ordinary except for the numbers showing its amount. It wasn't a one, a two, a five, a ten, or a twenty. Or even a fifty or a hundred. The numbers on the corners of the bill said 17. One-seven. S-E-V-E-N-T-E-E-N.

Vicky picked the bill up again. "I don't get it," she declared. "It's the best-*feelin'* green stuff I've ever held in my hands.

Perfect color, perfect printing, sharp points on the seal. Everything perfect except for the amount. What idiot would take the trouble to do all that, and then print 17 dollars on it?"

"An idiot who wanted to show me I'm a bigger idiot," Joey said gloomily.

"Naah, don't feel bad, kid. That kind of scam would grab anyone who hadn't been over the hurdles once." Vicky turned the bill over from front to back, looking at it closely. "Perfect," she repeated. "And believe me, I get to see a bunch of real toilet paper in here. Say, how about I give you a five-spot for this?"

"I'm hoping my boss will give me my money back when I explain what happened."

"Never happen," Vicky declared. "You're a dreamer. Better you should take my five and cut your loss."

"I don't think so, Vicky, but thanks."

"Come on," she said. "Sell it to me, okay? For ten? I want to include it in my deposit tomorrow. You know, listed separately. One 17-dollar bill. I can just see the frozen-faced looks on the tellers at the bank."

She waved the bill at Joey, "What do you say? A sawbuck?"

"Well . . . ," Joey hesitated.

"Great." Vicky pulled a roll of bills from her apron and peeled off a ten. She placed the 17-dollar bill to one side of the register. "I wouldn't want to mix it up with the rest of them in there," she said, smiling.

Four men came in and sat down at one

of the tables. One of them raised an arm to Vicky. She walked over to take their order. Joey took a quick gulp of his beer and put it down again. He slid off the stool. "Be right back," he called to Vicky.

He knew he wouldn't be.

Hit and move on. That was the way to work it. Hit and move on.

Out on the sidewalk Joey paused to check his watch. He still had time to take a run at the bar on the next block. He had checked that one out the night before, too.

The second place was also nearly empty.

The bartender was a young guy and seemed happy for the company. Joey selected a barstool. "Hi," he said. "I'm Joey."

"Ray," the guy said. "Mind showing me your license?"

They went through the familiar routine. Ray finally nodded. "What'll it be?" he asked.

"Beer." It had taken him twelve minutes to run through the tale with Vicky, Joey figured. It took him only eight minutes with Ray. The bartender placed the 17-dollar bill carefully in his pocket. Then he turned and walked down to the other end of the bar to wait on a customer.

Joey left his stool to go to the men's room. Just outside the door a hand gripped his arm. Joey swung around and saw the sharp-suited man who'd been in the other bar. Joey shook the hand off his arm, trying to remain calm. "What goes on?" he asked.

The man continued to block Joey's way. "Fallon, U.S. Treasury," he said. He flashed a gold badge in a leather case. "We've been checking out some of the stuff the bartenders around here have been coming up with. Let's have your wallet."

Joey handed it over. He was trying to keep the fright from showing on his face. "This should still be all right," he thought. But it was the first time anyone had caught up with him. Fallon looked through the wallet and came up with four of the 17-dollar bills.

The Treasury man waved them at Joey in triumph. "Where did you get this counterfeit, Mr.—uh—Quisenbury?" he demanded after looking at Joey's license.

"Counterfeit?" Joey asked. He kept his voice steady. "What counterfeit?"

"*This* counterfeit!" Fallon declared, waving the bills.

"What's being counterfeited?" Joey asked. He reached out and took his wallet back, leaving the bills in the Treasury man's hand.

"The currency of the United States is being counterfeited!" Fallon stated.

"Counterfeit is an imitation of an original, right?" Joey asked. "Show me the original of the U.S. currency you claim is being counterfeited," he continued before Fallon could answer. The agent looked down uncertainly at the bills in his hand. "What you have there, Mr. Fallon, is a one-of-a-kind item for collectors," Joey said.

Fallon shook his head stubbornly. "Don't try to doubletalk me. This paper. . . ." But then he looked at the numbers on the bills again. "You stand right here while I make a phone call," he ordered. "But I'll tell you right now, we're taking a ride downtown."

There was a pay phone a few feet away. After Fallon dialed, Joey walked back to him and tapped his arm. Joey pointed to the men's room door, then to himself. The agent nodded and turned around so he could watch the bathroom door while he was on the telephone.

The men's room was empty. Joey swiftly removed his suit and rolled it up. He bent down over the sink and scrubbed handfuls of water through his hair. That brought it back to its original dark red color. He also removed the makeup which had covered the freckles on his nose.

He removed his glasses and slipped them in the suit jacket pocket. When he came out, the rolled-up suit was under his arm. He was wearing his tank top and shorts. Fallon was arguing heatedly with someone on the phone. The agent glanced at Joey, didn't recognize him, then returned to his conversation.

Joey walked out the exit and down the street to his car. He smiled to himself thinking about the fake license. It had finally come in handy. Not only the picture of him in disguise, but the fake last name, too. He'd have to get a new ID now, of course. But at least no one named Monohan had been questioned about possible counterfeit money.

Flashing lights showed up in his rearview mirror. The siren was very persuasive. Maybe, Joey thought, it would be quite a while before he had a chance to see the look on Charley's face that said how proud he was of his only son.

DAN J. MARLOWE *is the author of more than 25 adventure and suspense novels. He's a past winner of the Mystery Writers of America's prestigious Edgar Allan Poe Award.*